CHANGE AUTHENTICALLY

A GUIDE TO TRANSFORM YOUR JOB AND LIFE THROUGH POSITIVE ACTION

ALLY BUBB

CONTENTS

Resources	vii
Introduction	1
1. Curmudgeons and Other Misery	5
2. Positive Action	19
3. The ACTION Plan	29
4. Positive Action for Life	47
5. Positive Action for Your Job	71
6. Those Who Act	93
Thank You	99
Acknowledgments	101
About the Author	103
Books by Ally Bubb	105
Notes	107

© Ally Bubb, 2020

All rights reserved.

The material in this publication is of the nature of general comment only and does not represent professional advice. It is not intended to provide specific guidance for particular circumstances and it should not be relied on as the basis for any decision on any matter which it covers. Readers should obtain professional advice where appropriate, before making any such decision. The author and publisher disclaim all responsibility for any liability, loss, or risk that may be associated with the application of any of the contents of this book.

Cover design by Erin Zastrow
Book formatting by Wolf Mountain Publishing

ISBN 978-1-952078-00-2 (ebook)
ISBN 978-1-952078-01-9 (paperback)

To the many miserable people working a job you hate – you deserve so much more than that.

RESOURCES

Throughout this book, I mention other books, links, and additional resources. All of it can be found at: WorkAuthentically.com

You don't have to worry about trying to remember any other links or the names of anything mentioned in this book. Relax and enjoy the process and focus on taking the right positive action for you.

INTRODUCTION

"*Since* we cannot change reality, let us change the eyes which see reality." – Nikos Kazantzakis

---

Many of us feel stuck in our current jobs but aren't really sure what to do or how to change it. I spent the better part of 20 years in the corporate world in both jobs I loved and jobs I loathed (once, they were even the same job!) and I've seen first-hand how hopeless people can become when they dislike their jobs. Regardless of where you fall on the love-it-or-hate-it spectrum and especially if you're feeling meh about your current work, know that it doesn't have to continue to be that way.

Once upon a time, I was incredibly naïve and made the incorrect assumption that things would somehow get better. I didn't know how, but I kept waiting and hoping. If you're in this camp, I'm sorry to be the bearer of bad news. It's not going to change unless you do something to make it change.

Not all of us have the luxury of working in a job where we can set our own hours or have control over the tasks we work on in any given day. In recognition of that, this book is a collection of actions you can take, even when you feel like you have no flexibility with your job/boss/company. I know what it is to be unhappy at work – it makes for long days and takes a toll on your body, mind, and soul, not to mention the impact it has for your employer because of the quality of work you deliver when you're in this state.

I will also point out that the premise of this book is that you can transform your world of work and beyond through positive action. I promise you, if you follow through on the advice, you'll see dramatic results. I also must point out that it may not be able to fix everything. If you are in a toxic company culture or one where you feel unsafe, you will need to take action immediately to address this. It could be talking with HR or it might mean cleaning up your resume and applying to as many jobs as you can find so that you can leave a bad situation.

The majority of the career coaching clients that I work with, and the majority of American workers in general, do not necessarily find themselves in such a bad place. There are people, policies, and programs that aren't great, but it's not all bad. There is good mixed in with it. Part of the issue is that we become so focused on the bad we lose sight of the good.

One way to immediately counteract the focus on bad is to take positive action and start a list of the good things about your job. How about getting a steady paycheck? Isn't that nice? I know plenty of people who would LOVE to be in that position! Do you have benefits? Then you're lucky! As a self-employed person, I sure do miss that aspect of my former corporate job. Do you have even one person you enjoy chatting with at work? Great! Add it to the list. Sometimes those small things don't seem like much, but trust me, writing down all the little seemingly unimportant good things goes a long way toward helping your brain shift your focus so you can see possibilities.

This book explores a wide range of topics from practicing interviewing to diet and meditation. The reason for this is because we can't separate our entire selves from our work and often when there are issues with work, there are also issues with other aspects or dimensions of our life. For example, if you are having relationship challenges at home, you are more than likely more emotional at work than when your relationship is going smoothly. All the elements of our work and life are connected, for good and for bad. The great news is that when you take positive action in life or specifically at work, other areas of work or life will also improve.

Some of what follows will make you nod your head and mumble to yourself, *"Well, duh. That's so obvious."* I agree. I have a friend and one of his top strengths is to say obvious information in a way that makes it sound like a brand new idea. It cracks me up every single time I hear it! But in the same way that common decency has become surprisingly uncommon in public spaces, I feel like I need to state the obvious for several reasons.

First, it might not be new news to you, but it may be for others, so I want to make sure everyone has the same foundation to build upon. Second, there is advice you've heard so many times that you've stopped listening to it. I know I have! So I want to make sure you not only hear the message, but that it is clear enough for you to take action since many of these strategies will make meaningful differences in your life. Finally, our lives have become an increasingly busy, frantic, race-to-the-end-of-the-to-do-list-so-we-can-start-another-to-do-list exercise in futility. Nurturing and growing your career doesn't happen without intentional action by you. It's way too easy to be caught up in the urgent and seemingly important minutiae of our daily lives and to blink and have a month, quarter, year, or even decade go by before we look up and wonder how we got where we are.

I speak from personal experience when I say that's a difficult and shocking way to wake up (more on that in a second). For now, let's try a fun exercise from the mindfulness world around setting an intention. An intention is basically the idea that you set the direction for your mind in advance and then allow the thing you see to manifest in your life. Setting a goal is future-looking toward something you want to achieve; setting an intention happens in the present as something you become. We'll dive more into the merits of meditation soon enough. For now, let's set our intention as follows: *I will try to see what may or may not have been obvious before with new eyes, open to the possibilities of how my positive action may transform my job and life.*

Doesn't that make it feel more positive and exciting already? Great! Now let's talk about misery…

1

CURMUDGEONS AND OTHER MISERY

"*Oh*, you hate your job? Why didn't you say so? There's a support group for that. It's called everybody and they meet at the bar." – Drew Carey

Unhappy Facts

According to findings from data in a recent Gallup study, only 15% of the global population loves what they do.[1] Hang on a minute! That means 85% of all workers in the world are bored, unhappy, disengaged, or downright hate their jobs. Surely it's better in America, land of opportunity, though right? Sort of. In the U.S., 30% of people love what they do. So that leaves a whopping 70% of U.S. workers unhappy.

Yikes. That means the majority of us are struggling on the daily. Trying to force ourselves to go somewhere and do something we don't enjoy. We're not able to use our strengths in a way that aligns with our authentic selves, resulting in misery.

I don't tell you all of this because I want you to feel hopeless. I mention it because I want you to know that you're not alone. They say misery loves company, after all!

One of the worst feelings I had when I was working a particularly terrible job was that I thought I was the only one who was so miserable. It heaped isolation and desperation on top of my misery because I didn't know anyone else was feeling the same way that I was.

It can be an incredible relief to know you're not alone. I would have loved to find others who felt the same way I did when I was so miserable. What the Gallup data is telling us is that we aren't alone.

Here's the data stated slightly differently. If you think of 10 people you know, 7 of them are unhappy and unfulfilled with their work. And yet, when we greet each other with a "How are you?" we all shout out "Fine. How are you?" We're not fine, though, are we?

The Gallup data shows that the majority of American workers identify with this feeling of misery, at least sometimes. But I'm guessing you didn't need the data for this to resonate – you wouldn't be reading this if you were able to work authentically, doing a job you love.

WHYYYYYYYYYYY?

fist raised to sky shouting into infinity (or as far as an angry human voice carries)

What causes this misery? It often comes down to three

dimensions within work: the specific job you're in, the team you're on, or the broader company culture.

When you're a bad fit for a specific job, it means you don't have the skills or interest to succeed in that role. It's not necessarily an indication that you're bad at every job, but this particular job is not a good fit. You can feel it throughout your day as you struggle to do the assigned tasks or you struggle to motivate yourself to do the assigned tasks. Either way, it's that feeling of struggle that characterizes a role mismatch. If you've been in that situation (as I have!), it is a miserable way to spend your day.

Sometimes, you enjoy the work that you're doing, but you don't enjoy the people you're working with (boy, have I been there!). This means a lot of your energy is being spent not on the tasks you need to complete to be considered "successful" on your annual review, but rather on emotional issues, drama, and disagreements. A dysfunctional team can be especially tricky to navigate, particularly if you would prefer to avoid conflict. Even if you are great at conflict resolution, addressing interpersonal issues requires a huge amount of mental and emotional energy. Speaking from experience, this can create abject misery!

Sometimes, the work is fine and the team is fine, but the culture of the company creates conditions of misery for employees (I've seen this in action several times too! Lucky me!!). This can run the gamut of experiences from massive layoffs creating instability to cost-cutting measures that put significant pressure on employees to work more (and more and more!) to the mistreatment of workers to company values that don't align to your personal values. The misery can be widespread throughout the company or in isolated pockets/teams/departments, depending on the specific culture issue.

Friends, I have even more bad news. The actions of your team, manager, and company are completely out of your hands. You can't control them. There is literally nothing you can do about them. But don't go giving up now! Here's the good news: The only thing you have control over is yourself. That's going to come in really handy soon.

There is a delightful concept from Stoicism around acceptance. Events that happen are neither good nor bad; they just are. It is only our reaction to the events that turns them into good or bad. We're passing judgment on the events largely because they don't line up with our expectations of what we thought/wished/hoped would happen.

If you want to learn more about Stoicism, I loved the *The Art of Living,* by Sharon Lebell, an interpretation of the works of Epictetus, one of the great stoic philosophers. In fact, I enjoyed it so much I bought two copies, one for each of my children, to give to them when they are older because I think it's indispensable advice on living well. I'm also hoping that it will be a book they return to over the course of their lives. The big advantage for them is that it isn't written by me and since we are often more open to advice from people who aren't our parents, I'm hoping it will stick!

Let's take the 2,000-year-old wisdom of the Stoics and bring it to a present-day example. I wasted tons of precious time and energy worrying about how things at work were turning out differently than my expectations. I was in a constant state of angst over the events of my day, replaying them in my mind, often wishing for a do-over. But the do-over never came and the angst continued to build. My reaction to the events was creating the dissonance in my life.

It made doing great work a lot harder for me because I was obsessing over how my work would be perceived by others (something I can't control). I don't know if you know this, but when you're focused on what people think, you can't be focused on putting your best work out into the world. Be smarter than me, sooner than me! I needed to learn to let that concern go and focus my attention on the things within my control.

In case you're thinking that came easy to me, it didn't! I spent the majority of my entire life in this state of anxiety. I have memories of worrying myself sick from before kindergarten. It took a lot of regular practice for me to move from fear and worry to a place of acceptance of things as they are.

Here's the good news: it's totally worth the effort! I am much more at peace and able to flow with things as they come my way since I stopped trying to pretend I could control them.

Curmudgeons

Curmudgeon *(noun): 1. a bad-tempered, difficult, cantankerous person*[2]

We all know someone who fits that description, don't we? Whether you work in a corporate office setting or a manufacturing floor, you've definitely crossed paths with that person. You might be stuck working with them right now, even! Curmudgeons are no fun (which is ironic, since curmudgeon is quite a fun word to say!).

We can label that curmudgeon as someone with a bad attitude, a pessimist, a glass-is-half-empty sort of person. Easy to say from our comfortable, non-curmudgeonly towers isn't it? But if we're honest, we all have our curmudgeon moments. I know I do! I've been difficult and cantankerous occasionally – just ask my family on any day when I haven't gotten a lot of sleep the night before!

Everyone has an inner curmudgeon. However, we don't always notice when our inner curmudgeon has been spending more and more time at work. The inner curmudgeon is sneaky. It starts with simple things, like complaining about all the ways other people are messing things up at the company. Of course, you need to vent and get things off your chest occasionally, but this is more than that. The complaining stops being a once-in-a-while vent and becomes a regular pattern. There is something to complain about every day, maybe every hour.

And then the inner curmudgeon goes further. It makes you feel put out that your great work is going unnoticed. It makes you mad (or scared!) at the latest round of layoffs. There is a sense of unfairness to it all. Next thing you know, you get upset at any new initiative that's announced, ready to tell anyone that will listen why IT'S NOT GOING TO WORK! Whoa! That escalated quickly, didn't it?

I've had times in my life when I had a bad attitude. Where I was a horrible curmudgeon, complaining about my circumstances. Poor me. The team/company/whole-wide-world is against me! I was focused on what wasn't working, instead of what was. Focused on the bad instead of the good.

Did complaining make me feel better? Maybe at first. But the more regular and habitual it became, the less productive it was. I had tipped the scales from venting to full-blown, in-your-face curmudgeon. And that, my friends, is no way to live or work.

The curmudgeon within causes us to perceive EVERY-THING that happens at work through that negative lens. We tell ourselves stories that <u>nothing</u> will change and it can <u>never</u> get better. We're spiraling out of control on how awful everyone and everything is. This behavior makes our situation seem worse and more hopeless, rather than filled with possibilities and solutions. One of the first clues that you're in this state is if you consistently use absolute language like always or never. If you catch yourself in this situation, it's time to pump the metaphorical brakes and immediately reflect on why you're feeling that way (I'll go ahead and step out on a limb here and guess YOUR JOB!).

<u>Not-So-Positive Action</u>

Our fast-paced, always-on world has endless ways to entertain us. And many of us use that as a coping mechanism. It's a whole lot easier to scroll through Pinterest for ideas of things you're never going to actually do than to try to get to the bottom of the mystery of why your job has you feeling so unfulfilled and miserable. Maybe you don't care about Pinterest, but you can't go an hour without checking your Twitter feed. Or Instagram. Facebook anyone?

Scrolling and scrolling and scrolling on social media fills time, but it doesn't fix the fact that your job sucks.

There's actually a long list of things just like that. I've tested many of these out for you already and I promise, any relief you feel is fleeting and the misery always manages to flood back in, often stronger than before. Let's explore a few more not-so-positive actions.

Shopping is a great one to hide behind. Our society wants us to be good consumers and to keep upgrading our stuff, so shopping is a socially acceptable and merchant-encouraged pastime that many people don't even question. Shopping as a numbing activity becomes a way to try to buy happiness. We feel a short burst of feel-good chemicals in our brains when we buy something new. We get a jolt of manufactured happiness when that new thing arrives and it provides the momentary relief we're looking for.

It's almost as if we're fulfilling a noble calling by fixing a problem (that marketers have implanted in our brains!) where we save the day by purchasing a trendy new living room set. *I'm a hero! I've done it! Applause erupts from the crowd!* That new living room is so amazing/wonderful/perfect/ beautiful/you/stylish. But then the momentary relief fades and we're back to where we were before, only a little worse off. *Maybe it wasn't a couch I needed. I'll bet it was a sweater. It is getting colder out after all.* And the cycle starts all over again. Shopping fills time and uses up your money, but it doesn't fix the fact that your job still sucks.

I love food! It can be both a necessity and a luxury and everything in between. It can also be another mechanism we use to try to stuff down our feelings about job dissatisfaction. That was 20 pounds ago for me. I started eating more at first to attempt to cope with stress. Then it was more for comfort to make the bad feelings go away. Then it was for numbing so I had something else on which to focus my attention. Eating fills you up momentarily, but it doesn't fix the fact that your job still sucks.

While we're at it, what goes best with food? Yes! Drink!! Or more likely drinks. For me, this one followed the same pattern as food. First it was to decrease stress, then comfort, then numbing. You have more than a case of the Mondays if you need to have a drink as soon as you get home from work. You know, before you can greet your family or eat dinner. As with all the other behaviors, drinking may help you temporarily forget, but it doesn't fix the fact that your job still sucks.

Overachievers, this one's for you! We wear BUSY as a badge of honor, partly so we can use it as an excuse to ignore the very thing making us miserable. When someone asks, "How are you?" we delight in answering, "Super busy!" rather than letting them know how bored and unfulfilled our job has made us. We think to ourselves, *"Maybe if I hit that next goal, this horrible feeling will finally go away."* And so you keep adding more things to the to-do list in the hopes that achievements and accomplishments will make up for the fact that your job still sucks.

Let's talk complaining. I'm the first one to say that sometimes, you need to vent and get all of your anger and irritation out in one fell swoop. But there comes a time, whether we're ready to admit it or not, that the approach stops being effective. We're venting about the same things over and over. Curmudgeon much? Yeah. The situation isn't changing. Your job still sucks. At some point, you have to be ready to try something new.

But sometimes, we keep these unproductive behaviors (and more!) around for no other reason than they are comfortable. We're so used to complaining about our job that we do it by default. We don't think before we grab that food or drink and throw it down the hatch. We're used to scrolling and shopping, shopping and scrolling, to pass any moment of the day that isn't accounted for. Of course, we've scheduled as much as possible into our days so we won't have any moment of free time, either. And we do it day-in and day-out, until we discover we're so numb that we don't really feel anything at all. When I was completely miserable in my job, I hated that non-feeling feeling the most.

Important Note: My lawyers tell me I should point out that I'm not a doctor, nor have I had any offers to play one on TV (yet!). The unproductive behaviors described above can also become addictive behaviors. If you think your behaviors might be on the edge between unproductive and addiction, seek professional help immediately.

Hold on! Something's still not quite right...

It's possible that the three sources of misery I shared didn't quite align with your experience. Maybe your job, your team/boss, and your company are OK. Or fine. Great even! Then why are you so miserable? There is something else at play that maybe you can't quite put your finger on. It's possible that you are even feeling some (or a lot of!)

guilt because you feel like you shouldn't feel miserable. I know I did!

I kept assessing my situation from a logical standpoint. I knew I was fortunate to have a job. That job paid me more than fairly for my work, even if the hours had become increasingly higher. I was benefits eligible. I had a retirement plan. I had some amount of flexibility and autonomy. There were numerous perks to the job. I should have been satisfied. Heck, I should have been thrilled! But I wasn't.

So what was the problem then? My logical analysis was correct. It was a great job. Unfortunately, it wasn't a great job for me.

I was spending all my time on energy-draining tasks I didn't enjoy and it was slowly crushing my soul. It's not always about logic or hours or dollars. You need to do meaningful work that you enjoy where you can be your authentic self with all your strengths and unique attributes. I wasn't able to do any of those things in that job!

Of course, everyone has bad days where you want to throw in the towel or secretly imagine storming out and quitting! And there will always be tasks you don't love as part of any job, but you shouldn't be waking up feeling dread. Every. Single. Day. That is a sign of misalignment. Here's what I mean.

The fundamental issue for me was that I had ignored my authentic self. I had pushed her aside and deprioritized her for years. I honestly didn't even recognize myself (not just because of the 20 pounds of stress-induced weight gain!). I hadn't been paying attention to what work I might really enjoy, or where I derived my energy, or how to best leverage my strengths and talents in service of things I cared about. I was completely lost. I had no ideas and no clear path.

And I knew I couldn't continue to be miserable in that job any longer.

At the end of the day, I walked away from a six-figure salary and a job title for one of the most marketable roles in my industry, with absolutely no plan or direction. I had a lot of fear. I had a lot of naysayers giving me "advice" through sharing their fears and doubts (in case I didn't have enough of my own already!). I had many people tell me I'd regret leaving. I had a lot of reasons on paper to suck it up and stay a little longer to "see if it changes."

But I was so sick and tired (literally and figuratively) of being miserable all the time.

All I had was a vague sense that there had to be something more and I was determined to figure it out. It's actually what led me to start my coaching and speaking business, Work Authentically. This misery that you're experiencing is the same misery I experienced. It stems from a lack of authenticity in your life and in your world of work. It permeates everything you do. And it's so hard to put a finger on, it's almost impossible to identify, at least at first.

We have two worlds that we constantly need to keep in alignment. Our inner realm includes our thoughts and beliefs about ourselves. In my inner realm, I'm a courageous heroine, doing good at every turn.

Then there's the outer realm. The place where things happen (some call this place reality). In my outer realm, I can get caught up in the moment and act like a total jerk as I yell at you for cutting me off in traffic.

In this scenario, the outer version of me (my action) doesn't align with the inner version of me (my belief). That misalignment makes me feel bad. And if it continues, that bad feeling becomes pervasive misery.

I have two choices once I recognize the misalignment.

1. I can change my actions to align more with my best self. This would involve me chilling out and not yelling or getting annoyed when I'm driving.
2. Or I can change my belief. Maybe I'm not the delightful do-gooder I thought I was.

So Now What?

We hopefully agree that not-so-positive action isn't the answer, even if it provides some form of temporary relief. So I'd like to suggest a different solution: positive action.

"Hey! This sounds like a book for optimists and that's not me." Cool. I welcome optimists, pessimists, Sierra Mists, really any kind of mist! The action isn't just for starry-eyed optimists, which is good, since they already have it made (right pessimists?).

The differentiator here has nothing to do with your worldview and everything to do with those who are willing to take action. Do you want to be the person who keeps doing the same thing every day hoping something will change? (It won't). Do you want to grow more curmudgeonly each day? (I hope not!). Or will you be the person who deliberately takes action to change all those things that aren't working for you?

Here's something you already know, even if you don't want to admit it: if you do nothing, nothing changes.

On the one side, there's comfort in that. Nothing will change. Hooray! And yet. You're miserable (or well on your way to becoming so or you wouldn't be reading this book!). Do you really want to stay miserable?

In my many corporate jobs, I've experienced both misery and joy. I assure you the joy is much more fun! Of course, you don't have to take my word for it. Try it for yourself! Implement even one small change and see how you feel. Slightly less miserable would still be an improvement, right?

As a person with many bad jobs under her belt, I have a lot of failed approaches on how to not fix your job. There are plenty of unproductive behaviors that I've tested unsuccessfully (or should it be successfully, since they were awesome at not working?!?) as my unwitting research for this book. It's basically an unflattering collection of some of my worst ideas. The best advice I can give you: Be smarter than me, sooner than me!

I want to help you skip past all those bad strategies and instead, share with you ideas of things that work. They worked for me, they work for my clients, and they can work for you too. That is, if you're willing to make changes. So, consider my experience to be the cheat codes you can use to be successful. Ready? Up up down down left right left right B A. (What did you expect? I spent 2 decades in tech!).

2

POSITIVE ACTION

"It's not hope that drives us into action, it's action that drives us into hope." – Rebecca Solnit

Positive

Positive *(adjective): 1. Constructive, optimistic, or confident 2. With no possibility of doubt; clear and definite*[1]

The end of December is one of my favorite times of the year, though not because of any of the traditional holidays you would think of. I love the planning and preparing for a new year. It's not the glitz and glamour and champagne of New Year's Eve that I love. It's the clean slate. A fresh start. A socially acceptable time to try something completely new and different than you've ever done before!

As a person who is frequently trying something new and different, I can safely say that people are much more open to that sort of thing for New Year's. It's a chance to dare and dream bigger and people are less likely to question your sanity. Of course, naysayers gonna nay, but for a short time around the first of the year, it's a little less.

For all my joy surrounding the end of the year, I've never been big on resolutions. In fact, I don't make them. Ever! It strikes me as odd that if a person discovers a big change they want to make in July, that they would then wait until January to follow through on it. I'm a big believer that when you find something you want to improve, you should take positive action immediately!

On the other side of the resolutions-spectrum, maybe there's no major change you feel like you need to make in January. So why would you expend the energy trying to come up with some resolution to do (that you're likely not fully committed to!) just to appease those who want to know what your resolutions are? There's nothing worse than trying to accomplish something you think you "should" do instead of something that you truly desire for your authentic self. It's a recipe for a failed resolution.

If you enjoy the ritual of making resolutions and have found ways to be successful, by all means, continue. I know that's not the case for most of us. So I'll suggest an alternative.

First, let's talk positive. On any given day, there are lots of actions you can take to achieve any number of results. Not all of those actions are positive.

Here's an example. In December, my car broke down unexpectedly as I was driving my two kids to an appointment. I'm grateful I was able to maneuver safely to the shoulder of the road, getting out of the way of the rush hour traffic. It was frustrating and inconvenient to be stuck. Both the tow truck and my improvised ride home (my wonderful spouse!) were over 30 minutes away. It would have been easy to fall into a whole bunch of not-so-positive actions (complaining, getting out of the car to kick the tires like they do on TV, etc.). In the moment, I had a choice: I had to ask myself what positive action I could take instead.

I should point out that I am not mechanically inclined, so opening up the hood (however you do that!) and working on the car wasn't a positive action available to me. Given the volume of traffic whizzing by us, walking elsewhere was also not viable. I had recently (within that same week, in fact!) downsized my gigantic holds-a-thing-a-majig-for-every-possible-scenario mom-purse into a tiny, stylish wristlet, so no entertainment or answer (or even snack!) was going to be found in its 8" x 6" confines.

You'll notice the improvised feasibility study I did on the aforementioned options included a quick assessment of my strengths and abilities. Working on the engine-y stuff could absolutely be a positive action for someone with those strengths. Lacking in the know-how and ability meant I could quickly rule this possibility out. The same will be true for you as you seek out positive action. Identifying the perfect action (fixing my car singlehandedly) does me no good in the real world if it doesn't align with my skill set.

I needed to find a choice that aligned with my strengths, interests, and current supplies on hand within the confines of my stranded car that also lived into the definition of positive. *Constructive, optimistic, or confident*

I decided that the three of us would use our quiet time stuck in the car to build the ultimate holiday music playlist.

I will point out that we could have taken on this activity while being angry and bitter. We had to make sure we were doing it in a constructive, optimistic way.

The playlist did several things.

1. Provided a much-needed distraction from our present circumstance (and don't we all need that sometimes?!?!).
2. Created an opportunity for us to get to know each other better. We could ask questions like "What made you pick that song?" or "Is that your favorite artist?" and all sorts of other questions.
3. Allowed us to get started right away, amidst our imperfect conditions. We didn't need to wait until we were in the mood to create a playlist. We didn't need to feel inspired. We just needed to start doing it and see what developed.

As can be the case with positive action, we had a blast taking turns picking favorite holiday tunes and singing along as we added each one to the ultimate playlist. It was a fun way to spend close to an hour. Added side benefit: we may have a new holiday tradition now!

Singing didn't get us out of our trouble any faster (contrary to what musical theater would have you believe!), but it made our time spent a lot more enjoyable. It's a small example of the myriad ways you can incorporate positivity into whatever action you're doing every day.

By contrast, the following evening after a series of stressful events, I made a less positive choice in a conversation with that same wonderful spouse who had willingly agreed to come to rescue me from my broken-down jalopy less than 24 hours before. So yeah. That happened.

Turns out I'm a wonderfully flawed human, which comes as no surprise to anyone who has ever met me! Needless to say, I had to reset my attitude (after I apologized!) and move forward.

The point of both examples is that it's a journey. Our default reaction may not always be the most positive thing. Acceptance of that fact, as the Stoics just reminded us, helps us to be more kind to ourselves and others when we screw up (which we will!). It also helps us remember to keep validating that what we do at any given moment contains a positive element.

Action

Action *(noun): the fact or process of doing something, typically to achieve an aim*[2]

If you made it here, you're at least willing to consider trying a more productive, positive approach to creating change at work. Again, you need to remember that you have absolutely NO CONTROL over your team/co-workers or your company's actions.

I found it to be really freeing once I finally stopped trying to control all those things that are out of my control. It helped me move from a state of constant worry into a much more intentional and relaxed person. For anyone that knew me in my younger years: sorry about all that misdirected intensity!

The thing we can control is our own action. What we

choose to do or not do is where we should be spending our energy and effort.

We've talked about the fact that when we do nothing, nothing changes. So instead of nothing, we must to do something. It doesn't have to be a monumental something. It can be the smallest sliver of something. But we need to take some sort of action to effect change.

I am constantly looking for ways to improve. It's one of those facts that is central to who I am as a person. The desire for improvement is not just focused on myself, but on systems, processes, even my physical environment. Because of this tendency, I've read a whole lot of self-help books. All. The. Books.

Here's the thing, though. The knowledge is absolutely useless without corresponding action. If I know what to do and never actually do it, I will not get the improvement I read about.

We all know how to be skinny – eat less and exercise more. We all know how to be rich – spend less and save more. Yes, I'll grant you this is an oversimplification of what goes into both of those things, but the point here is it's not the knowledge we lack; it's the action.

If only it were as simple as reading a healthy cookbook and now my eating habits could be transformed. Instead, I have to take the action of buying new and different ingredients and preparing a new recipe. I also have to choose NOT to eat a container of cookies later in the day. There are lots of actions required by me to make this change.

It takes courage to try something new. To do something that you've never done before. To be willing to take a chance in the hope that you'll finally get a different result.

For me, I had to get to the point of abject misery before I was willing to do something new to transform my job. Be smarter than me, sooner than me! Don't wait until you are completely miserable.

I've experienced in my own life what a difference it makes when you're doing work you truly enjoy and I want to help you do the same.

Positive Action Framework

Positive *(noun): constructive, optimistic, or confident*

Action *(noun): the fact or process of doing something, typically to achieve an aim*

Positive Action *(noun): the constructive, optimistic choice to change authentically, resulting in the realization of small and big aspirations*

Doesn't positive action sound like fun?!?!

Positive action can be considerably harder to choose than the default choices of inaction or not-so-positive action. However, when our positive action is aligned with our authentic self, the choice becomes much easier. You're becoming the person you believe yourself to already be by taking the action. It brings harmony to your inner and outer worlds.

You're probably wondering, *"How in the world do I go about infusing my authentic self into my action planning?"* I'm so glad you asked! We're going to walk through the Work Authentically ACTION plan that gives you the tools to ensure your positive actions are aligned to your authentic self.

Positive action is an iterative process. We try something

small, learn from it, and react to the information we've learned. It follows this pattern:

Action —> Assess —> Adjust

Action: Identify a positive action to improve a dimension of your work or life.

Assess: Take the action and see how things have changed.

Adjust: What adjustments do you need to make to continue to see progress? What new action should you take? (which starts the cycle all over again!).

Here's the example of when my car broke down and we created the ultimate holiday music playlist.

Action: Have youngest person in car pick a song and add it to a new playlist. Sing-along and dancing optional, thought highly encouraged, as it plays.

Assess: Is this activity worth continuing? Yes! Are we having fun? Yes!!

Adjust: Have next youngest person in car pick song. Continue.

We can also see how it works with not-so-positive action, like the day after my car troubles when I chose a less constructive approach.

Action: Say something mean to your spouse.

Assess: Did it have the desired effect? Maybe it did, but… Was it a positive effect? Nuh-uh. Did it improve the relationship? Nope. It actually made more work for me since then I needed to…

Adjust: Apologize!

Yes, it really can be that simple. Try something small. See what happens. Make an adjustment and do it again. The point is to keep taking action without getting bogged down by trying to plan everything out from now until you retire. When we take the plan-everything approach, it's easy to get overwhelmed and then most of us, myself included, take no action. Starting small is key.

Positive psychology has had an exponential growth in popularity and overall, that's a wonderful thing. I also believe that while our thoughts are extremely powerful, they aren't the only thing for us to rely on. The positive gets you so far, but it needs to be coupled with action in order for you to be truly successful. You need action to implement the changes you want to see in your life and your work. And because change is hard, it's critical that you see progress quickly, rather than in days, months, years.

To that end, for the rest of this book, you'll see concepts and ideas to try out, along with at least one **#PositiveAction** you can complete in a matter of a few minutes so you can immediately begin to move forward. Of course, it's not possible to put every single idea for positive action into a short, actionable, easy-to-read book. The ideas are designed to get you started, help you continue your journey, or be the spark you expand upon within the context of your own life, job, needs, wants, preferences, and the like.

For anyone struggling with feeling inauthentic and the misery that stems from it, there will also be ideas in the ACTION section to **#ChangeAuthentically**.

I encourage you to go to WorkAuthentically.com to download a Positive Action Guide so you can capture the positive actions you are inspired to take to transform any aspect of your job and life you feel would benefit from it.

As we've talked about, taking positive action is the tool

everyone has available to them. And positive action will transform your job and life. We're going to dive deeper into the elements of ACTION next.

#PositiveAction to try, continue or expand

- Find one action today that could benefit from positivity and make the intentional choice to engage in positive action. If you aren't sure where to start, ask yourself these questions:
- How can I make this activity more fun?
- How can I be helpful to someone else?
- What does a better outcome look like?
- Where do I see a person or situation that I could improve?
- How can I use this to bring me one step closer to a dream I have?
- Share your journey with me on social media. I love to hear stories of how people #ChangeAuthentically and take #PositiveAction.
- Twitter: @workauthentic
- Instagram: @workauthentically

3

THE ACTION PLAN

"*Often* people attempt to live their lives backwards: they try to have more things, or more money, in order to do more of what they want so that they will be happier. They way it actually works is the reverse. You must first *be* who you really are, then, *do* what you need to do, in order to *have* what you want." – Margaret Young

---

Positive action has the power to transform our jobs and lives, especially when we harness that power for maximum results. Maybe you're thinking, *"Positive action is way better than the not-so-positive action I've been taking up to now."* And you're right. It is.

It's also more effective when it's part of an intentional plan for change. I've seen the dramatic results of this in my own life, as well as in the lives of the clients I work with.

Incorporating a plan will help you get where you want to go faster than engaging in random positive actions.

I like to keep things simple wherever possible, so if you can remember the acronym ACTION, you'll be able to remember what to include in your action plan. It stands for Aspiration, Consistent, Targeted, Identity, On Purpose, and Next Steps. Let's dive in, shall we?

Aspiration

Aspiration is another word for dream; a desire to achieve something. I believe it's one of life's greatest joys to bring a dream to life. Of course, a dream doesn't get you where you want to go. Positive action does!

I have a chair in my house that is my dreaming chair. It's a 15-year-old recliner that my two cats absolutely adore. It's the place I go when I want to guarantee some snuggle time with them. It's also the place I go to slow down and let my mind wander.

As humans, we need both time and space to dream. Creating the physical blocks of time in your daily schedule (yes, daily!) is critical. So is the white space that is created when you have no other distractions, obligations, or activities during that moment of time. In our over-scheduled, always-on world, one of the most productive things you can do is nothing, even if it's only for 5 minutes. Use this as the permission you've been waiting for to kick back and let your mind wander for a few minutes!!

My creativity has been significantly higher over the past year, partly because I've deliberately given myself the time and space for dreaming. Sometimes I hop in my dreaming chair and nothing much happens, other than sitting there. Sometimes I get an idea to solve a problem whether for my business, a client, or my family. Sometimes, I get the inspiration for my next big project! I never know what the outcome will be and I don't have any expectation for it. What I can say with certainty is that I feel renewed and ready to tackle the next task on my list after I'm finished.

You might be wondering how to do this in your daily life. It's 3 simple steps.

1. Schedule the time, whether 5 minutes or a whole day off from work, it's up to you.
2. Actually use the time you scheduled. It's one thing to write down something on your calendar. It's another thing entirely to do the thing that's on your calendar. So hold the time you scheduled.
3. Turn off electronic devices and distractions. I promise, all the work and demands and notifications of the world will still be there a few minutes from now. Be careful, you might find you actually enjoy uninterrupted time!

When you follow these steps, you'll start to dream more. You'll come up with amazing Aspirations! Sometimes, it'll be change-the-world Aspirations, like impacting a million or more people in a specific way. Sometimes, it'll be a simple, change-the-moment thing, like eating healthy food for the rest of the day. The dreams can be all shapes and sizes. The only rule to the dream is that is HAS to be authentically yours.

#ChangeAuthentically

- Start a list of Aspirations for yourself. If it's been a while since you've spent any time dreaming, don't be surprised if nothing springs to mind immediately. Be patient. Start a list to capture Aspirations any time one comes to you.
- Review your list of Aspirations regularly. What new Aspirations do you think of as you re-read them? Are the Aspirations authentically you? Should anything be removed from the list?

In the context of positive action, your actions should be focused on leading you toward your Aspirations. Keep asking yourself, what's one small step I can take today toward my Aspiration? You may feel like you have almost no time to devote to it, but there's still something small you can do each day. If you do that consistently for a month, you'll be surprised to see how those 30 actions got you further than you imagined possible! And speaking of consistent...

Consistent

Our culture loves to tout the 3-simple-steps-you-must-be-doing-right-now solution to every problem. I'm here to say that contrary to what the click-bait articles would have

CHANGE AUTHENTICALLY

you believe, it's more about consistency. Consistent positive action is what helps someone lose 200 pounds, not eating one salad for lunch one day. Consistent positive action to save money (made more powerful by compounding interest) is what turns an average person into a millionaire. And Consistent positive action will transform you and a job you hate into something completely different.

A long time ago, in a galaxy that didn't have streaming video (or even DVDs yet), I had a workout video where the host would say something to the effect of, "Consistency is the key to results. See you tomorrow." I still think about that video now whenever I hear the word Consistent!

We tend to dismiss the importance of consistency, but if I learned anything from that ancient workout VHS tape, consistency really is the key to results. Isn't that disappointing? We can't do something once and expect to see major change. I know I consistently (see what I did there?) struggle with that very real fact. I can't eat one salad and be considered healthy. I have to consistently choose the salad over the French fries with a side of mayo (try it before you judge!).

All the people who regularly use a gym HATE the month of January. There are a whole lot of well-intentioned people hanging around trying to crush their new year's resolutions. The gym is a crowded, uncomfortable place to be at the start of the year. Luckily for the regulars, gym attendance is back to normal by Valentine's Day when the majority of people have given up on achieving their fitness goals.

Consistency is needed in any area of your life that you're trying to improve. If you're trying to grow a business, you can't sometimes work harder at it. You need to consistently work toward that growth. It's the same if you're trying to change the direction of your career. Sure there are easy things you can do in 5 minutes or less, but you also need to consistently (aka regularly) work toward the change that is your Aspiration.

Here's something to consider. Being Consistent is also a promise to yourself. Once you've got your Aspiration, that dream worth chasing, you're making a promise to yourself that you are willing to make the dream happen. It means you show up and do what you need to do. It means you schedule the timeline to "30 days from now" (not "someday") and stick with it.

Unfortunately for many of us, we deprioritize what's important to us in favor of doing something that is important to someone else. Sometimes that's generous, but more often, we're afraid of doing what we need to do and use busy-ness as an excuse to never get around to our own Aspirations.

I spent years in reprioritization mode, never having time to work on my Aspirations. Here's what I learned: the more you don't work toward your Aspirations, the less likely they are to happen!

Shocking, I know.

So be smarter than me, sooner than me.

If you're struggling with this, you may want to get the help of an accountability partner to move forward! This is a person that will speak the truth to you in love because they genuinely want to see you succeed. This person will support and encourage you, but also will ask hard questions if you're getting off course from your Aspiration or not being Consistent to make it happen.

#ChangeAuthentically

- What promise do you need to make to yourself to bring some consistency to your Aspirations? It's time to regularly work toward what you want!
- What timeframe are you setting to achieve your Aspiration?
- How often will you work toward your Aspiration?
- Who do you know that would be a great accountability partner to help you make progress and keep the promise you've made to yourself?

<u>Targeted</u>

Once upon a time, I had the worst year of my entire life professionally and personally. That story is too long for today, but suffice it to say that it helped me realize that I was not choosing to live or work authentically. I came to the conclusion that almost nothing was working for me in the way I was approaching my life. Whoa! That's kind of a big, complex problem, huh?

It's definitely not the sort of thing you can fix in a single day (or even a single year, but I made, and continue to make, progress!). What's the solution? I had to get Targeted in my action. I couldn't fix everything all at once. I needed to focus on the most important thing.

One of my favorite things to do for the new year... *drumroll please!* ...is to clean out my closets! I know, I know. It's a wild and crazy life I lead. Here's the thing: It gives me a chance to clean spaces that don't get cleaned very frequently, but more importantly, I can assess the stuff I own and ask questions about it. *Does this fit AND flatter?* Or *Does this serve the current life I lead?* Or *Have I used this enough in the past year to warrant expending my time and space to keep it here?* Annual closet cleaning sure is sounding a lot more fun now, amirite?!?!

My inner Clutter Conqueror would love to go through the entire house like that. Asking questions, cleaning out all the rooms from top to bottom and ending with a space that even Marie Kondo would be jealous of. But my real life doesn't afford me the time or energy to do all that. Not to mention the fact that with a family of four this Zen-like space I'm imagining would be back to a mess in 5 minutes flat.

One choice I could make is to say, "Well, it's pointless. I might as well not do anything." Another choice I can (and do!) make is to say, "What is a Targeted approach where I could achieve that Aspiration on a smaller scale?" This was how my tradition for cleaning out my closets for the new year was born!

I focus my attention on one area, knowing there are lots of other things that could use my attention, energy, and effort too. But I prioritize this activity because of several reasons.

First, it's small, which means I can accomplish it in a short amount of time. I love to see progress quickly! Next, it helps me let go of all that other stuff I could/should/wish I had time to work on. Freedom from guilt! Finally, as a recovering perfectionist, it gives me great joy to have a few small spaces of order in the chaos that is my daily life. If you've never spent a minute or two gazing upon a well-organized space, you absolutely must try it! Talk about relaxation!!

Hang on... I think I'm getting slightly off topic. I must be more Targeted! Yup. That happened!

As I've mentioned, resolutions aren't for me. I love change! I just take a different approach to getting there. One of those different approaches is to select a word of the year.

I've been doing a word of the year for the past five years. Some of my previous words include: Grateful, Listen, Release, and Enough. There are lots of people who advocate a word of the year, so if you're curious, give it a try!

What I love about a word of the year is it's Targeted. It allows me to keep my focus on one thing for the year. At first, I thought it would be hard to spend a year with a single word, but I have been pleasantly surprised every year by how the word continues to take on new, different, bigger meaning in my life. The fact that it's Targeted is what makes it so effective.

When you're thinking about taking positive action, you want your action to be Targeted. It's easy to get overwhelmed when you think of all the things you'd like to change or do or be. By making a choice to focus your time, energy, and attention on one thing, it becomes possible to make incredible progress!

#ChangeAuthentically

- Identify the one thing that is most important for you this year. The Targeted attention will be transformational!
- What boundaries do you need to set to ensure your action is Targeted?

Identity

When it comes to leading an authentic life, one of the big challenges comes in around clarity. Many of us, haven't spent enough time figuring out what matters most to us. Or maybe, like me, you've spent a lot of time thinking about this very topic, but the answers that you've surfaced don't ring true. There is the strange sense of misalignment between what we think and what we do, but we don't have clarity on the connection points between those two things.

At this point, I would be remiss if I didn't mention a particularly vile and destructive word, commonly used in the English language. SHOULD.

Should is the enemy of your Identity. *Should* is a barrier to being your authentic self.

Should makes us feel guilt, shame, and a sense of obligation to do or be something that we don't want. And *should* is very sneaky – we often don't notice we're using it.

Should disguises what we enjoy and what's worse, gives us a false sense of being noble when we do something we think we *should*.

Imagine, if you will, a hypothetical example. It's late on a Thursday night and my child tells me at bedtime they need a snack for school tomorrow. I sigh and say, "I *should* make cupcakes." I have no earthly desire to make cupcakes. I have no interest. I have a sense of obligation to provide a snack. Making the cupcakes will not result in anything other than misery for me, even if it provides some amount of enjoyment for others. I only thought I SHOULD take on this activity because it's what a "good mom" would do. It's the "right thing" to do. Stale pretzels (the only thing left in the pantry) will be judged by the other kids/teachers/parents.

And this is how *should* gets us to do things. It makes me worry about things outside of my control and guilts me into doing stuff I don't really care about. Watch out for *should* as you work to create actions in alignment with your Identity. Your goal is to find the person you are, not the person you feel like you *should* be.

There are other factors beyond *should* that can also create challenges in the Identity piece of the ACTION plan. I have a tendency to be a people-pleaser. For me, enduring my own discomfort is far more palatable to me than seeing others unhappy. Besides, I was used to being worried and uncomfortable, so it didn't seem like a big ask to continue to feel that way. And so began one of the ways that my authentic self began to disappear. I was allowing others to choose what made them happy and going along with it, rather than choosing what would make me happy. Eventually, it got to the point where I didn't even know or recognize things I would enjoy anymore.

This one small personality quirk (people-pleasing) was one factor that created the sense of misalignment in my work and life. I share that story to help you see that inauthenticity can occur as a result of circumstances, personality, challenges, choices, and many other factors. Regardless of how we get there, we can also choose a path toward alignment again.

So how do we go about this act of recovering our authentic selves? Or how do we make sure that our ACTION plan is authentically aligned? There are two key pieces that we'll explore.

First, let's talk about the best version of you. The version of you that you imagine you are. You know, the one that you want to be, before the craziness of modern living wreaks havoc on that plan! What characteristics does your best self embody?

Second is to assess (or review, if you've done this already) your values. You are authentically you when your values align with your actions. Each person's values are different and unique to them. They can change over time. For example, until I had some health challenges, I didn't realize how much I truly valued good health. My actions dramatically changed when I prioritized health. To get started on assessing your values, you can do an internet search for a values exercise, or you can download one for free at: WorkAuthentically.com.

Any positive action you're taking needs to help bring you closer to your best self and to your values. On any given day, there are millions of actions you can take, so ensure your actions are creating the alignment that's been missing.

As can often be the case in a journey of discovery, you may need to spend time introducing the best version of yourself to you. It may take time to recognize the wonderful authentic you that's been waiting to be acknowledged. Once you do that, you can then introduce your best self to the world so you can live into it.

You'll know you've got this part right if you find yourself saying, *"I want to meet this person because they sound amazing."* Yes they are. It's you authentically.

One client shared that same sentiment as she read her resume. It made her feel interested, impressed, and a little awestruck to see her work accomplishments articulated so clearly. Be prepared to be wowed by yourself too!

#ChangeAuthentically

- Spend some time determining your values or review your list if you have already done an exercise. Do you need to make any adjustments to your list?
- Are your actions in alignment with your values?
- What characteristics does your best self embody?
- Are your actions bringing you closer to your best self?
- What SHOULD do you need to let go of to live and work more in alignment with your values

and best self? It feels amazing to let those unrealistic expectations go!

On Purpose

Entire books have been written on the importance of finding your why. I will not rehash all of them, but I will agree with the fact your why, aka being On Purpose, is a key element of the ACTION plan.

Until you have a compelling why driving you to achieve an Aspiration, you're unlikely to take meaningful steps to get there. This is the reason so many new year's resolutions fail. Without a why, we lose interest. We can't stick with the change. The why is our motivation to be Consistent and keep taking positive action.

Even if you and I have the same Aspiration, it's highly unlikely that we would share the same why. When I'm taking positive action On Purpose, it reflects my unique experiences and interests; yours will too. My why would likely not motivate you because our experiences are different.

Let's take exercise as an example. The reason I exercise is because I want to walk unassisted when I'm in my 90's, just like my great uncle. For another person I know, their why is because many of their relatives died at younger ages and they exercise to hopefully not have the same happen. For another, it's that they want to continue to fit into their current clothes so they don't have to buy new ones. There are endless why's for something as simple as choosing to exercise. The key is to find the why that is true for you.

Another way to think about your why if you're struggling is to determine what you stand for or against. This is often a meaningful reason that leads into a compelling why. My family has been significantly impacted by cancer, so I support causes and engage in activities around finding a cure. I also have a love of the natural world and the environment, so again this helps me direct my energy toward volunteer efforts.

In a world where we have unlimited choice and access to information, being On Purpose also helps to narrow your focus and stay Targeted. You can easily filter out those positive actions that are good, but not aligned with your Identity or your why and what you stand for (On Purpose).

#ChangeAuthentically

- Why do you want to achieve the particular Aspiration you identified?
- What benefits do you hope to get from your Aspiration?
- What do you stand for? Against?

Next Steps

As we've discussed, positive action is an iterative process that follows the Action/Assess/Adjust framework. As you learn from one Next Step, it will inform the rest of the Next Steps you take.

If your Aspiration is to get a new job in an industry

you've always dreamed would be fun to work in, you don't want to plan out every possible step from now until you retire from that job. Instead, try something smaller, like researching job descriptions to compare your current skill set to your desired role. What did you learn? What will you do next?

This is the fun of the Next Step! I love that it is a manageable chunk I can quickly and easily do. It goes back to the old (and somewhat gross!) adage: *How do you eat an elephant? One bite at a time.*

The same is true for each of us. How do we achieve our Aspiration? One Next Step at a time.

The intent is not to find the most perfect thing to do; it's about testing, learning, and moving forward. It's easy to get paralyzed by the sheer number of choices when you're looking for the perfect thing, so if you find yourself struggling with this step, try to think about the absolute smallest thing you can do. It might be so small, it seems insignificant, but when done consistently, it'll become significant progress.

Each Next Step is something that brings you closer to your Aspiration, while maintaining alignment with your Identity. Remember that the best Next Steps are small and something you can do quickly to assess progress and make any needed adjustments. The point here is to avoid getting too far down a particular path before discovering you need to course correct.

#ChangeAuthentically

- What is the smallest Next Step you can take toward your Aspiration?

- How many different Next Steps can you think of? Which ones are best aligned with your Identity? Do you need to break any into smaller steps so they are more Targeted?
- What Next Step will help you find out an important piece of information quickly?
- Can you complete your Next Step in an hour or less?

4

POSITIVE ACTION FOR LIFE

"The life we want is not merely the one we have chosen and made. It is the one we must be choosing and making." – Wendell Berry

---

You know that hilarious notion that each of us can leave our personal lives at the door when we get to work and ignore all those other things happening while we focus on delivering high-quality, emotion-free work? It's absurd. And it's impossible. Sometimes we pretend we can compartmentalize work and our personal life. You may even know some people that appear to be good at doing this. Unfortunately, it's an unrealistic expectation that no one can live up to all the time.

Sometimes, the misery we feel that we associate with our job actually stems from the non-work-related areas of our life. When I don't feel my best, I can't do my best work, plain and simple. It took me longer than it should have to see how my own action (or frankly, inaction at times) was interconnected to my misery and lack of fulfillment at work. All of my not-so-positive behaviors were contributing to making me feel worse about myself, my job, and my life. Be smarter than me sooner than me!

The other piece we absolutely must keep at the forefront is that any change you make must be authentically you. Doing something because someone else said to do it is NOT a compelling why, nor will it help you to live On Purpose. You know what you want to change or have at least some idea of the areas of your life that are working better than other areas. Each of us must decide for ourselves where we will focus our efforts to change authentically.

Let's look at several of the ways that improving life in general will also improve your job.

Take better care of yourself, starting today

No really. Starting today. I mean it! Again, I'm not a health practitioner or a doctor, so I'll point out that you should consult with someone in the medical field when considering making changes to your health. As I tell my clients: You are an expert in YOU. You know what's best for yourself. Onward.

If you're like me, you're probably thinking some version of, *"I take pretty good care of myself"* or *"Well, I'm not in as bad of shape as so-and-so..."* This is the part where you need to get brutally honest with yourself. Are you really taking good care of yourself? I have a great uncle who is in his 90's and I am constantly reassessing my progress in light of a milestone like that. Am I consistently making the choices that will help me live well when I'm in my 90's? I have to keep working on all those things to which the answer is not yet yes (there's still lots of room for improvement!).

I know this area is a struggle for most humans. We logically know what to do. It's better to pick the carrot over the donut. It's not a lack of knowledge that's slowing our progress. It's about behavior. Even when I was feeling my worst, I knew I needed to find a way to deal with the stress more effectively. But all those numbing behaviors were routine and comforting, and a whole lot easier than trying something new. My brain was overwhelmed with enough stress, without trying to figure out a better path.

I tried and failed at a lot of systems and programs designed to help me change my behavior. I'll share the way of thinking about this topic that has worked for me, but it might not work for you. That's ok. Keep searching until you find something that does work because selfcare is the most radical, powerful, life-changing gift you can give yourself. The all caps shouting should show you how seriously you should take this concept.

As part of my journey to get clarity around how to re-architect my life, I came across a simple concept from behavioral consultant, Nicholas Bate who says we should daily be "giving consideration to M-E-D-S or meditation-exercise-diet-sleep.

Wellness is about balance. M-E-D-S is a simple such strategy.

M is meditation. Take a bit of time out. Just to think.

E is exercise. Walk every day. Walk more. Take the stairs.

D is diet. Reduce the rubbish; increase the nutritious.

S is sleep. Get rid of sleep debt."[1]

Back when I was in my miserable curmudgeon state, I was out of balance on all four dimensions. I was "too busy with work" to make time for meditation or exercise. I was eating to numb the pain rather than to fuel my body. Sleep was the worst of all for me, though. I couldn't fall asleep due to stress and the fact that my body hadn't been overly active all day. I would wake up in the middle of the night thinking about something I needed to do at work. And then there was that whole alarm-clock-dread thing happening where I didn't want to wake up and go to work. I was a mess! If this sounds like you, take heart.

A friend went through similar health challenges at roughly the same time as me, but she took a different approach than I did. Her approach worked for her, even though it didn't work for me. I bring this up not to say there is any one correct path, but to highlight there are many paths leading you where you want to go. The key is to find the path that is best aligned with you authentically.

I made the choice to intentionally focus on my health as a first step toward the change I knew I needed. My Aspiration was simple: stop feeling awful. I committed to myself that I would be Consistent and take positive action every day. The MEDS gave me a framework to be Targeted so I didn't feel overwhelmed. My best self is vibrant and active, so this aligned with my Identity. I am On Purpose when I'm making choices that will help me live well in my later years (hopefully well into my 90's). My Next Steps were very small typically. Eat one more vegetable than the day before. Walk one minute longer than yesterday. You can see how those would quickly add up to big things!

By incorporating the MEDS into my daily life and I've noticed a dramatic difference. On the handful of days I haven't felt good in the past year, every single time, it was because I had forgotten to focus on my MEDS the day before and I could feel the difference (for example not getting enough sleep or eating less healthy food). Small adjustments helped me get back on track quickly and these days, I'm far less likely to sacrifice my own health to try to accomplish anything else. Does this mean I never have stress or challenges or bad days at work? No. But when I take care of myself, I'm a lot more resilient to the stress and challenges and anything else that comes my way. I can't do my best work or live my best life if I don't feel my best. Be smarter than me, sooner than me!

#PositiveAction to try, continue or expand

- Assess how you are doing on each of the MEDS to get a baseline. Keep track of your meditation, exercise, diet, and sleep for a week and see where there is room for improvement.
- Spend some time envisioning your best self. What does this person do differently than what you are doing today?
- Pick one dimension of the MEDS (such as Sleep) and take the action necessary to bring

that dimension back into balance (like go to bed earlier).

Meditation

There are roughly a kajillion apps that you can download immediately to get started with meditation. You don't even need an app. All it takes is to sit somewhere, close your eyes, and focus on your breathing. No tools, no guide, no fancy expensive trip to India to become more mindful. Just breathing (which you were probably going to do anyway!) and focusing on that breathing. Many workplaces also offer mindfulness or meditation classes. And I'm sure I don't need to remind my fellow introverts just how magical 20 minutes of uninterrupted silence can be. These days, I deliberately set my alarm early, just to experience the restorative power of silence before my family wakes up. Regardless of what or when it is, find something that works for you so you can stop doing and start being for even 5 minutes.

#PositiveAction to try, continue or expand

- Download and try a meditation app such as Calm, Simple Habit, Insight Timer, Headspace, or Meditation.
- Schedule 20 minutes of uninterrupted quiet time on your calendar and then keep that commitment to yourself!

- Wake up 5 minutes earlier than usual and use that time to meditate.

Exercise

Some people truly love exercise. And then there are the rest of us. We do it because we have to or we avoid it because we haven't found a way to enjoy it. I didn't even like using the word exercise because I had so many myths, beliefs, and baggage wrapped up in that term! I had to get around those negative emotions by shifting my thoughts to ensuring I had activity every day. Activity felt less formal, scheduled, and exhausting than "exercise" and it felt a lot more doable for me, especially starting out. I could walk for 5-10 minutes between meetings. I wasn't willing to commit to setting my alarm at 4:30am to go to a gym and do some sort of routine. If that's your thing, great! Keep up the good work! If it isn't your thing, try something else! There are lots of ways to incorporate more activity into your day.

#PositiveAction to try, continue or expand

- Walk for 20 minutes a day. The average male will burn an extra 700 calories per week simply by adding in this activity. A brisk 20-minute walk daily also lowers your risk of heart disease by 30%. Plus it improves mental focus and sleep

quality.[2] In 20 minutes! Productivity hack much?!?!
- Park farther away – I know it's cold/rainy/windy/snowy/sunny where you live, but humans were designed to be outdoors. Take the farthest spot in the parking lot and enjoy not only the benefits you'll get from walking, but also pat yourself on the back for doing a good deed since now someone who truly needs to park closer can find a space.
- Can you do a push-up? I know I couldn't when I started incorporating activity into my days! See how many (or few!) you can do in 30 seconds. Use this number as your goal to keep improving.
- Research the gyms near where you live or work. You can get a tour to see if it's something you might enjoy. Some gyms also offer childcare!
- Some companies offer on-site fitness centers for reduced cost or free. Check it out if you are lucky enough to have this benefit!
- Think back to the activity you loved when you were a child. Maybe it was running, playing on the monkey bars, riding your bike, or swimming. Find a way to do one of those activities and see it's still something you enjoy.
- I heard a nurse speak at a conference and she shared the best exercise tip I've heard. People ask her all the time, "What's the best exercise?" Her response, "The one you'll do consistently!"

So find something that works for you and then keep doing it.

Diet

Diet can be especially polarizing around what's the best or easiest or trendiest approach to try, so let's go ahead and save everyone time: you can skip the angry emails about the food groups or the ideal mix of micronutrients! I'm not interested in that debate. Instead, let's all agree that what you put in your body as fuel has dramatic effects on your body.

I struggled to stick with a lot of different eating programs until I landed on the simplest version that works for me. And like with exercise, what's most effective is what you'll actually do. The simple answer for me is to eat more vegetables and fruits than any other thing. I've mostly cut out gluten and sugar because they don't make me feel good. I've significantly reduced dairy for the same reason.

I never feel bad on days when I eat enough vegetables. I'm not a vegetarian, but I definitely consume less meat than I used to, again because of how it makes me feel. The idea here isn't to find something super restrictive that you do for 6 weeks, only to go back to your old eating patterns. That's not sustainable, nor is it going to deliver lasting results. It's not about goal weight or dress size or anything like that. And it's not about the number on the scale because that number on its own is arbitrary and meaningless. The way I know I'm successful is based entirely on how I feel. When I feel healthy, I do better in work and life.

#PositiveAction to try, continue or expand

- Assess your current diet. Write down everything you eat for a week and review the results. You may be surprised at what you see!
- Contact a licensed nutritionist to talk about your diet. A nutritionist can help recommend changes to achieve your long-term goals.
- Talk to friends or co-workers that are successful in maintaining a healthy diet. Ask them what they are doing so you can learn and try it!

Sleep

There's tons of great advice on how to sleep better (just like all the other dimensions). Remember, it's not about knowledge, it's about putting that knowledge into action! Consistent sleep is truly one of the best gifts you can give yourself. It's the exact thing your body and mind need to function optimally! I used to think that sacrificing sleep and the resulting exhaustion was a badge of honor that showed how hard I was working. All it really showed was that I wasn't taking care of my body the way I need to! Be smarter than me, sooner than me!

#PositiveAction to try, continue, or expand

- Go to bed and wake up at the same time every day.

- Don't use your phone (or any other screen) 30 minutes before bedtime.
- Find a relaxing nightly ritual – I like to unwind with a cup of caffeine-free tea. You may find you prefer quiet music, aromatherapy, or reading. Whatever it is, do it consistently to help trigger your body to get ready to fall asleep.
- Activity - I sleep a whole lot better on the days when I'm active… if your sleep is off, double check your E dimension of MEDS, to make sure that you're getting enough exercise/activity.
- Sleep meditations – sleep meditations are an incredibly effective way to relax at bedtime. Plus, sleep meditations are a great way to combine meditation AND sleep as you drift off to dreamland. We're a society that loves productivity hacks, so go ahead and do more in less time, by being instead of doing!

There are lots of reasons and excuses for why we don't take good care of ourselves. The problem is we can't do our best work if we fail to do that. When you practice consistent selfcare, many of those stressors that are annoying you daily will start to look diffcrent. You might be surprised to discover how much your current job transforms when you actually feel good!

Sign up for a class

I know what you're thinking. *"I don't have any spare money to sign up for a class!"* We'll be talking about finances shortly, but there are also plenty of options that don't cost a dime. And I know you're also thinking, *"I don't have time for a class!"* Agree. You're probably swamped with work responsibilities that are making you miserable. I'd argue that you will benefit the most from doing a little less work and spending some time in a class.

Where to begin? Go to your local library. You know, that place that houses more books than most people could ever dream of. Books. You know, those things that people used to carry around for entertainment before they had computers in their pockets. Ugh. Never mind.

But seriously, go to your library! Most offer free or very low-cost classes on a variety of topics. In the past year, I've been to library classes on Zentangle, the history of the tea ceremony, basics of essential oils, reducing clutter and helping the environment, and mandala rock painting. There are frequently special programs for children as well as adults and I'd highly recommend you spend some time exploring a topic that you've always been curious about (or maybe never even heard of!) to learn and grow.

I have several friends that are naturally curious and they have been great at modeling the behavior of regularly taking new classes. Sometimes, it's helpful to observe and/or ask others how they've been successful at something. If their tip aligns with your authentic, best self, by all means steal the idea! For me, it means scheduling the class in advance. I'm far less likely to attend if I didn't schedule it and it's at the end of a busy workday. For other people, it's the opposite and they don't want to be tied down to a schedule. Find something that works for you in all your uniqueness!

As for professional development classes, check and see what your company offers. Many companies offer classes and speakers on leadership throughout the year. You can also look up conferences specific to your industry or job. Many employers will pay for you to attend, particularly if you are willing to share the information you get with your team when you return. No skipping the sessions for a free vacation – your company is paying for this! Take good notes and bring back ideas on how your team and company can put into action the knowledge you've just learned.

That said, if you have a choice between two flights and one allows you more time before or after the conference to explore, go for it. You need a little selfcare too!

I had never been to New York City and had the opportunity to attend a conference for work. It was a tight schedule, but the first conference session on the first day didn't start until 10am, which gave me time to explore Central Park, stroll down 5th Avenue, and stop by 30 Rock all before the conference doors opened. Was it my dream New York vacation? No. But it was fun to see a few of the iconic places that I'd seen featured in TV and film. Plus, I had lots of stories to share with the attendees at the conference (most of whom did not take advantage of the opportunity) and it made starting networking conversations easy and interesting.

The internet is great for lots of things (and also terrible, depending on where you're looking!), but one of my favorites is the democratization of knowledge. Basically, you can find information and online classes on pretty much any topic ever invented... and new ones are being invented each day. It used to be much harder to find people interested in (or even aware of!) hobbies outside the mainstream like building trash sculptures, but today a simple browser search or smartphone assistant question will bring you back loads of information on anything. Even if your company doesn't have the budget for a multi-day, cross-country trek to a conference, most companies will support you taking an online class that will improve your skills.

#PositiveAction to try, continue or expand

- Spend a few minutes searching for a topic online that has always interested you and isn't related to your job.
- Find an online class and sign up! If you don't know where to start, try Udemy, LinkedIn Learning, or Khan Academy.
- Practice the pitch you will give to your boss when you ask to attend a conference. Make sure it includes the value/benefit the company will get from your attendance. Run it by a trusted friend or co-worker for feedback before you take it to your boss.

Find a Tribe

Remember that time we talked about how the internet can also be a great/terrible communication tool? That was awesome! You can also use it to find a tribe of people to learn from who are interested in the same things you are.

There are lots of reasons to find a tribe. Several books, including Seth Godin's *Tribes,* Brené Brown's *Braving the Wilderness: The Quest for True Belonging and the Courage to Stand Alone,* as well as any basic psychology book that covers the topic of *Maslow's Hierarchy of Needs* will explore this concept if you want to dive deeper. But in the same way that I am helping you jump the line on career success, I'll tell you what I know here.

It's human nature to crave belonging. As humans, it's one of our top needs.

A tribe is one way for us to meet that need for belonging, as long as we can be authentically ourselves as part of the group. If you're part of a group and feel like you need to act in a way that doesn't align to your values and best self, then it's time to find another group. Your need for belonging won't be met if you're not authentically you.

I am also a big believer in belonging to more than one group. My career trajectory changed significantly for the better when a friend invited me to join a mastermind group with him. Our group met monthly and that meeting served as the necessary accountability for all of us to take action in between meetings to make sure we saw the progress we wanted in our careers. It also gave me a great support network where I could bounce ideas off my fellow group members. They shared their very honest, sometimes-hard-to-hear feedback with me on anything and everything. It changed the way I approach work and life and I am still in close contact with most of them today, many years later.

I didn't invent the concept of a mastermind group. That goes back to at least 1937 where it was shared in Napoleon Hill's book *Think and Grow Rich.* While we're at it, I didn't even invent the idea to start the mastermind group I was lucky enough to be invited into. I'm grateful to my friend for taking the initiative. Be smarter than me, sooner than me and get a group!

#PositiveAction to try, continue or expand

- Join a group with a shared interest of yours. This could include work topics or it could include something that has nothing to do with your work, like art, the environment, team sports, a book club, etc.
- Think about the people you've most enjoyed working with during your career. Ask two of them to create a mastermind group with you and have them each invite two highly respected co-workers. High five yourself and the rest of your new group for taking the initiative!

<u>Start reading</u>

What's that? You're already too busy to add one more thing? Great! This is about removing something that isn't (always) adding value to your life! Technology.

I'm not talking about removing all technology, all day (although, I do highly recommend a regular digital detox). I'm talking about 30 minutes a day. You've probably already spent that much time just watching hilarious cat videos on YouTube today… or was that just me?!?!?!

We all have the same twenty-four hours each day (if all goes well!). Each time I wonder how a certain person "has time" to do something amazing, I need to remind myself that I have the same amount of time. It's about what I'm spending my time on that differs from them. So then, it's about actively choosing what you care about vs. passively scrolling on a screen to see the latest updates from online friends on stuff that likely doesn't matter much in the big scheme of things (I'm talking to you, pictures of people's dinner!).

I'd read for years that cutting out screen time in favor of reading would produce positive results in my life, but for various reasons, I wasn't ready to make the change until a few years ago. It's been amazing! I've learned more, been entertained more, and frankly have enjoyed life more since I started doing it.

#PositiveAction to try, continue or expand

- Give up only 30 minutes of screen time a day and see what a difference it makes in your life. I'd recommend the 30 mins before bedtime, since the light from screens messes with your sleep, but as a person with a business, a family, and a whole lot of interests, I know how hard that can be. I'm all for you stealing time wherever and whenever you can! If 30 minutes feels like a Herculean effort, start with 10 minutes a day. You'll still be amazed at the progress!

- Hate reading? You're in great company! Lots of people do. You can listen to books and learn without ever having to crack one open. Try audible.com to get started.
- Book listening too long (or boring!) for you? No problem! All the big authors go on popular podcasts to talk about their books. To find one, you can search podcasts by topic, author, etc. Download one and listen on your commute to work. Optional step: Laugh smugly to yourself as you think about all those people reading the whole book while you got the summary in a fraction of the time!

Volunteer for work you find interesting

I know. You don't have time for volunteering (or taking classes, if I remember correctly). You're going to do that when you retire and have more free time. How do I know? Because I was going to do that too!

Here's the best advice I can offer on the topic: Don't wait. This is as critical as selfcare because volunteering helps you as much as your volunteering is helping someone or something else. Volunteering helps reduce stress, create connection, and improve mood, among other amazing benefits.[3]

Volunteering is also a great way to enhance your resume and LinkedIn profile while learning new skills (for free!). You can showcase leadership, time management, and a variety of other valuable skills gained or honed through volunteering.

Also, there's something to be said for the contentment of saying you made a small difference in the world. The best way to get out of a bad mood is to help someone else, even if it's as simple as buying the coffee for the person behind you in the drive-through. The next time you're out of sorts, do the first kind thing you can think of (hold the door, tell a joke, give a compliment) and see how your world shifts to be more joyful.

And who doesn't have time for more joy in their lives? I know my joy and fulfillment has significantly increased since I began regular volunteer work.

#PositiveAction to try, continue or expand

- Start a gratitude journal where you write down 3 things you're grateful for each day. Re-read when you need a boost!
- Do a daily random act of kindness (which, by the way, fits into everyone's busy schedules!). Search for "random acts of kindness ideas" if you're not sure where to start.
- Find an event for a local charity group doing work you are interested in and sign up. Put it on your calendar so you have something to look forward to! Better yet, sign up with a friend to double your impact and fun.
- Look at your skills and see how you can offer that to a charitable organization near where you

live or work. Nearly every non-profit needs help from people with specialized skills like computer/typing, organizing, filing, answering phones, greeting/talking to people. There is likely something you're already great that would be a huge help to a group!

Create some financial margin (aka get out of debt!)

What in the world do my finances have to do with my career and WHAT BUSINESS IS IT OF YOURS ANYWAY?? The mere mention of discussing finances brings most Americans to caps lock shouting pretty quickly. And I know this feels a little unrelated to positive action around your career but hear me out. Most of us go to work because we have to, not because we want to and we work now to pay for things we bought in the past (sometimes things we don't even own anymore!). Every month we send our hard-earned money to the credit card companies, car lenders, student loaners, and a whole host of other places.

There is an element of desperation around people with debt. I nickname it "needs it too bad" syndrome, which isn't catchy, but is accurately descriptive. Watch almost any reality show today and it'll be easy to tell who will not win. It's the person with the hardest story; the one whose whole life turning around hinges on winning the prize money from the show. I love pointing out when someone "needs it too bad" as they weep into the camera.

Not because I enjoy seeing people struggle! I actually

hate that part. It's because my brain likes to figure out who's going to win/turn out to be the killer/guess the plot twist as quickly into watching a show as possible. Can you believe no one wants to watch TV with me? Weird, right? Good thing I stopped watching so much TV and started reading more! Anyhoo…

Try it next time you're watching a reality show. All you have to do is find the one who "needs it too bad" and you can spoil the results for everyone! Of course, after you've spoiled it for everyone, you'll likely be celebrating that victory watching TV alone, but it's a victory none-the-less.

Let's move from "reality" TV to real life. Everyone has met a salesperson that is a little too eager to make a sale and although you may want to help that person, you are also a little (or a lot) turned off by that desperation. It's the overly eager person working on commission; the person who lost their job suddenly and needs a new one to continue to make ends meet; or the kid who needs to hit a certain amount on their fundraiser to go on a special trip. You've seen the "needs it too bad"/desperate salesperson many times in many forms.

So what does all this have to do with getting out of debt? At times in our lives (maybe even right now), we've ALL been that person, where the results mattered so much more to us. Where we just HAD to hit the number/earn a certain paycheck amount. And just like you can sense it when you run into people who need it too bad, other people can sense it in you.

On the flip side, when you don't have monthly payments to make to a bunch of banks, you suddenly have a little breathing room in your budget. You can weather some uncertainty or emergency without it being a major issue. You become much more relaxed when you aren't constantly worrying about money and paying bills and an almost magical transformation happens. You no longer have to make career decisions solely on the basis of if they can sustain your debt burden. You have infinitely more possibilities around what you choose to work on and with whom, simply because you removed the variability of monthly payments.

There are millions of personal finance experts and I don't claim to be one, but I will share my personal story because I think it highlights all of the points above.

The best way I found to get out of debt was to follow the advice of Dave Ramsey. Nothing else worked for me the way his best-selling *Total Money Makeover* book did. He and I disagree on nearly every topic, but for some reason, the process in his book clicked for me in a way that no other personal finance advice had.

Like many Americans, I had poor financial habits and a lack of basic financial literacy. I didn't realize the damage I was doing to my financial future by buying everything on credit. I had a vague sense that I was making decent money but it always felt like I had none left over at the end of the month. I was working very hard at jobs (some of which I enjoyed, others not so much) but had nothing to show for all my hard work.

It was a very shocking and painful wakeup call when I finally pulled together a list of all my debt and it was close to $100k! I was scared and didn't know what to do, but by using the plan outlined in Ramsey's book, I was able to pay off that consumer debt in roughly 2 years.

Again, I'm not a personal finance expert and I have no interest in comparing the merits of one strategy vs. another – there are more than enough of those voices available for you to seek out already – but the experience was transformational for me. I no longer felt the stress and strain of payments. I was unburdened. Free.

And for the first time in my life, that allowed me to make career choices based on what I WANTED TO DO instead of what I NEEDED TO EARN. If you are struggling in a job you hate strictly based on payments you must make, consider doing some research to find a debt-reduction program/philosophy that works for you. You'll be amazed at how your career options open up when you are no longer the one who "needs it too bad."

Even if you love your job and you're never planning to leave, you'll be glad if you take this step simply for the peace of mind and wealth-building opportunities it will create for you. Speaking from personal experience and the experiences of my clients, eventually every job becomes untenable for various reasons (new management, change in strategy or policies, reduction in staff, your interests change), and you'll be especially thankful you followed through on this strategy.

#PositiveAction to try, continue or expand

- Make a list of everything you owe and assess how you feel about that number.
- Choose not to buy one thing today that you were

going to buy (coffee, lunch, a sweater, a car!) and save that money instead.
- Find one voice in the personal finance space that resonates for you – there are lots of blogs, podcasts, and other resources. Try search terms like "personal finance expert" or "financial freedom."
- Take one step recommended by the personal finance expert of your choice today. And do it again tomorrow.

5

POSITIVE ACTION FOR YOUR JOB

"We can't take any credit for our talents. It's how we use them that counts." – Madeleine L'Engle

As we continue down the path of exploration together seeking possibilities for ways to change authentically, I want to again mention that as unique and wonderful individuals, we all have different talents and strengths, interests and insights, values and principles, and priorities and responsibilities.

Indeed, you know best what's going well and what's going poorly with your job. In my many corporate jobs, the same was true for me. We sometimes default to the easiest answer of *I need to find a new job* when there are problems with our current job. While that can be necessary sometimes, there are also many positive actions we can take to improve our jobs *without* getting a new one.

Clarify what's working and what isn't

Have you ever stopped to notice what you enjoy and don't enjoy about your job? Many of us get to the state of misery without ever noticing those tasks and interactions that are slowly depleting our energy. By the time you're miserable, all you want is a quick escape (the not-so-positive actions) or a new job (there's a good chance you'll feel the same eventually at the next job without clarity).

Many people are grossly unhappy at work but honestly have no idea why because they haven't taken this step. Don't skip this. Don't skim over this by saying, *"I'll do that later because I don't want to get up for a pen and a piece of paper right now."* You won't do it later, no matter how well-meaning you are! I've read more self-help books than most people and have been the skipper, skimmer, maybe-I'll-make-that-list-later person a bunch of times. Be smarter than me, sooner than me!

Life is always a choose-your-own adventure, so you can decide how to approach getting clarity. You can dive in right now or schedule an hour yet this week. You need only a pen or pencil, a piece of paper, and yourself, with no distractions, so you can be brutally honest. And remember, this isn't an exercise in complaining. The intent is for you to see on paper what isn't working for you so you can make changes.

For some people, it's hard to capture all their misery at once, partly because our brains don't always remember all the things that happened during a work week. Many of my clients find it easier to spend 5-10 minutes at the end of each workday noticing how they feel and writing down those things that were particularly enjoyable or painful from the day.

Within a few days, you should see a pattern around what tasks, activities, and interactions are not working for you. You may see that your list contains a mix of things related to your specific job duties, your team/manager, and your company as a whole. Or everything on your list may be related to one dimension, such as your manager.

Next, it's time to assess the list. Are the things you hate about your job things you can change? Or have no control over (other people's actions, company direction, etc.)? Rearrange your single list into two lists, with one side being things you can change and the other side being things you can't. Practice some Stoicism and vow to stop being mad/frustrated/annoyed over the things you can't change. Your job will feel a lot less stressful when you let that go.

Then, it's time to take positive action on the things you can change.

Job-specific

When the activities that make up your day-to-day work existence are unenjoyable or even misery-inducing, your days feel long. I've been there (several times over the course of my career!). As much as you feel stuck, know that there are positive actions you can take to make it better.

. . .

#PositiveAction to try, continue or expand

- Talk to your boss to see if the tasks and activities that are draining you are necessary. Sometimes, we keep doing something because we've always done something and the need for that task may no longer exist. Note: Don't do this for every single thing on your list. Your boss will not respond positively if you ask to stop doing your ENTIRE job description! Start with the one or two things on the list that are most burdensome for you.
- Then, if the answer is that the task/activity is still needed, it's time to brainstorm solutions for how else the work could be done (By someone else? In an abridged way? Through a new mechanism?). For example, maybe a senior leader needs/uses a small piece of information on a report you have to prepare regularly. Could you deliver only the small bit of information rather than the full report? Take time to make sure you are approaching this problem solving from a place of openness and willingness to deliver value to your company. You will find there are a surprising number of possibilities when you do this.
- How can you take a boring task and make it fun instead? Sometimes, we have no choice in life but to do something unfun, like washing dishes, so you need to find a way to approach it in a way that changes it from drudgery to something

enjoyable for you. Let's use the dish-washing example. You could listen to music or a podcast. You could spend time in gratitude thinking about the meal you just ate, or being grateful for the many people that have been served on that single dish, or a whole host of other things. You could set a timer to see how fast you can wash the dishes, working toward a personal best every single time. With all these suggestions, the task of washing the dishes didn't change. Only our approach and our mindset around it did and that task stopped being so horrible. The same is true for your boring work tasks.

Team/manager-specific

If you are struggling with your manager or team (or both), it could be that it stems from a lack of understanding about each other. It's challenging to work with a person that seems to approach work in a way that's dramatically different from you. Often, it's a lack of understanding or clear expectations that can be corrected by getting to know each other better.

#PositiveAction to try, continue or expand

- Suggest to your manager that your team take an assessment tool and then talk about your results together. Some good starting points: Myers-

Briggs Type Indicator (MBTI), Clifton Strengths, or *5 Languages of Appreciation in the Workplace*
- Offer to organize and run a monthly meeting where you talk as a team about what you learned in the assessment and how you see it manifest itself in the workplace. Yes, this is more work for an already busy and overburdened person, but you may find that it starts quickly improving your relationship with your team and manager, which will greatly reduce the burden you've felt up to this point.
- Suggest to your manager for the team to do a book study on a topic that would be helpful for everyone. It could be related to the type of work your team does (marketing, customer service, etc.) or unrelated (diversity & inclusion, productivity tips, etc.). The point here is to create a deeper shared experience through reading and discussing a book so you can learn from each other and grow as a team.
- If your challenges are with a particular person, start to cultivate a positive relationship with that person. I know! It's the last thing you want to do – spend more time with someone that drains your energy! But the sooner you can find common ground, the less painful your day-to-day work life will be. Invite that challenging person to coffee or lunch and show genuine interest in them. As much as we tell ourselves that a person we don't like is dramatically

different than ourselves, the fact remains that we're all human and we all have more in common than we think. Ask questions about where they grew up, their work philosophy, their pets, anything to get them talking! Then genuinely listen. Keep looking for your common threads rather than your differences. I guarantee you'll find something!

Company

If most of your issues are with how your company deals with customers, values (or doesn't value!) employees, and the products they provide, then there's no positive action you can take, right? Guess again! This is one of those areas outside your control, but there are always things you can do.

#PositiveAction to try, continue or expand

- Join an employee affinity group doing work you want to support. It could be around getting more women and underserved populations into leadership; it could be around providing feedback to management on the employee experience. If you can't find a group like this, start one!
- Some companies spend a lot of time creating an updated mission, vision, and strategy and then

fall short on how to execute on it. That's great news, since it means this is an opportunity for you to step up and lead! It doesn't have to be changing the company singlehandedly, but you can offer to bring this to your team and work together to genuinely come up with a plan for how you'll contribute to the strategy. It's a simple thing, but the more tied we feel as individuals to what our company does, the more we enjoy our jobs.

- Do you have ideas on how to make something at work better? Share them with your company! Many workplaces have programs where you can submit improvement ideas, and if one doesn't exist, figure out who to talk to in your organization. All companies are interested in saving time and money, so any idea that does that (plus makes your work life better) is a win!

Define Your Personal Brand

In the same way that we don't always stop to clarify why a particular job isn't working for us, we also don't always stop to think about what it's like for other people to work with ourselves. At its core, that's what personal brand is. It's a perception held by someone else on the experience of working with you.

Each of us possesses strengths, skills, life experiences, and more that contribute to how we approach the work that we do. This is why even when two people are hired to fill the exact same job description, you get different results. There are lots of ways to be successful and reach the targets set for a particular job. Each of us leverages our unique strengths, skills, life experiences, and more in order to do our best work.

If you've never thought about your personal brand (or were secretly hoping it was a fad that would go away!), don't despair. The simple question to ask yourself is, "How do I want to be perceived?" This brings us right back to the fact that we can't control other people's perceptions. So what can we do? Bring the focus back to you and your positive action.

The only thing you can control is how you show up to work on a consistent basis. Maybe you're the go-to person for solving problems. Maybe you're the empathetic listener that makes people feel heard. Maybe you're the energetic leader of discussions. Whatever it is, YOU get to decide what it's like for people to work with you based on your actions every day.

Chances are good you already have some idea of what people think of your personal brand because they've told you. This comes in formal feedback/reviews sometimes, but more often in casual conversation where someone thanks you or compliments you for something you did well or shares an idea around how you could improve. A long time ago, in a work galaxy not-so-far-away, this was known not as your personal brand, but as your reputation.

Your personal brand is extremely valuable and should be treated as such.

. . .

#PositiveAction to try, continue or expand

- Take time to figure out what your personal brand is. Think about the compliments and feedback you've gotten at work. Then add in anything else you want around what you'd like people to experience in working with you.
- Assess your actions at work. Do they align with your personal brand that you've defined? If not, change your approach to one thing yet this week.
- If your actions align with the brand you've defined, think about ways you can start to amplify your brand. It's as simple as reminding your boss of the awesome job you did on that last assignment or sharing on a social media tool how you took a class to get better on a particular topic.
- If you haven't been bringing your best self to work lately or if you have been struggling with job/team/company challenges, you will need to give your personal brand extra attention. This could include improving on something (like getting to meetings on time instead of late) or resetting expectations with people ("*I know I haven't done this consistently in the past, but I'm working on changing that this quarter*"). People are often willing to help if you share with them an area that's been a challenge for you.

Seek Out Mentors and Sponsors

One of the best things you can do for your career is to seek out mentors from every age and stage of life. I'm a firm believer that everyone has something to teach and something to learn. So find some people willing to share their wisdom with you!

Not sure where to start? Look within your company. Is there anyone that you admire, someone who does amazing work, someone with a job you'd love to have someday? Reach out to them and ask if they'd be willing to try out a mentor relationship with you. If they say yes, you need to be ready to do some work. Come to your meetings prepared with questions or a problem you'd like their input on. You may find you enjoy your job a whole lot more when you've got a mentor that supports you and is invested in your success.

It's also helpful to cultivate a mentor relationship outside of your company. That person will have a completely different perspective on events and changes happening within your organization. Plus, you'll have another source for wisdom and advice by meeting with someone external. This could be a former boss or co-worker, neighbor, or maybe someone you meet at a random dinner party. Regardless of how you know them, show up prepared for those meetings too.

A sponsor is someone who is willing to advocate on your behalf. They are actively using their positional authority and political capital to recommend you for new roles and help you advance in your career. This person is often at a higher level on the organization chart.

Finding a sponsor differs from finding a mentor as you need to have developed a relationship with a more senior person at your company. This takes time and won't develop overnight, but it is worth investing in so you have multiple people helping you along your career journey. Again, look for someone you admire and/or who does great work and invite them to coffee as a starting point.

#PositiveAction to try, continue or expand

- Find one mentor inside and one mentor outside your company. Meet at least quarterly.
- Prepare for your mentor discussion! Write down questions to ask them around work, approaching a specific challenge you might have, leadership philosophy, etc. They are willing to help you get better, so show up with discussion items that will help you do so!
- Invite a senior leader you admire out to coffee to start building a productive relationship. Be respectful of their time and prepare for the discussion.

Consider a Coach

If you're feeling particularly stuck in your job and unable to focus on possibilities or take positive action, you may need to consider getting a coach. This is someone that can talk with you and help you get unstuck so you can move forward. If you like what you're reading, you can contact a Work Authentically coach for help!

There are times in everyone's life where we need someone to coach us through small (and sometimes big!) moments. Here's an example. I've struggled for most of my adult life with consistently flossing my teeth. I was a sometimes-flosser, not a daily-flosser. *Gasp!* I know. I was familiar with the lecture from the dental folks I only had to see twice a year on how it's important and healthy and blah-blah-blah. I knew the right thing to do. I was lacking in the action department.

When you see dental floss commercials, they always show someone flossing as they get ready for bed. Same on TV sitcoms. I naturally assumed that the only time of day to floss was right before bedtime, since that's what I'd seen. Here's the issue. I'm a morning person. I do my best work and have my highest energy in the morning. At night I'm tired (and sometimes grumpy!) and have no interest in expending effort on… well, anything… but especially flossing!

Enter the dental hygienist who successfully coached me through the issue. I shared with her that I was a morning person and was too tired at night to floss every night (a lame, but very true excuse). Instead of telling me I should try harder or that it's important and healthy, she gave me an easy positive action to take. Floss at the time of day that works best for me.

Wait. What? Do it when it's convenient for me? Like pretty much everyone else in the world, I LOVE things that are convenient for me! How has this idea never been mentioned before?!?!

Pretty simple (and obvious), right? But it had never occurred to me because I believed flossing was part of a bedtime routine. That simple insight to get me unstuck completely changed when and how often I floss.

Unless you're in the tooth cleaning industry, this probably sounds insignificant. It's just a little more minty freshness in the world. No big deal. But it was the exact insight I needed to finally take positive action to do something different to get a different result.

The same is true for a coach in any other aspect of your life. They will ask the hard questions and point out the sometimes obvious insights to help you get unstuck. It's one of my favorite parts of working with clients when I can help them move past an issue that's been holding them back. Remember, coaches come in all different forms, sometimes with an official title, but more often in the form of a friend or co-worker or dental hygienist willing to point out an alternative course of action for you to try.

#PositiveAction to try, continue or expand

- What's that small thing you've avoided changing, even though you probably know what to do? Find a way to reframe by asking a friend for ideas to get unstuck.
- If you're feeling especially stuck, find a coach that specializes in that thing and start working with them.

- Not sure where to look? You can search the internet for specific types of coaches depending on what area you're feeling stuck. Try terms like financial coach, career coach, life coach, etc.

Practice interviewing

Just because you may not need a new job today doesn't mean you should completely ignore the day when you will eventually apply for a new job. If you're like most people, you don't enjoy interviewing and you get nervous. When we're nervous, we often unintentionally make a poor impression on one or more of our interviewers.

The takeaway? Don't wait until the pressure is on and you're interviewing for your dream job! Instead, practice interviewing now, when it's low risk and you have nothing to lose. The best time to think about interviewing is NOT when you have an interview starting in a few minutes.

You can start out simply and research common interview questions. Then, practice your answers to them. Better still, have a friend ask you the questions and practice your responses out loud. You'll never regret being overprepared to tell your best story.

Plus, it comes in handy, not just in interviews, but when you meet people and talk about what you do for a living. That is your chance to practice telling a compelling story – don't waste it saying your job title! You can practice sharing your personal brand whenever you're getting to know someone. This is great interview prep because you can experiment with weaving your personal brand into your answers to the questions the new person will be asking you, similar to how you would approach an interview.

It's a free and easy way to get comfortable telling your story to others so that when the pressure is on, you will feel confident!

#PositiveAction to try, continue or expand

- Research common interview questions and practice your answers to them.
- Keep a running list (digital or on paper) around the big challenges and accomplishments you've had at work. This alleviates stress in an interview when the interviewer asks you for a specific example. Your brain won't freeze up in the moment when you know you've got that info at your fingertips.
- Set up time to hang out with a friend so you can both practice interviewing. You can use those common questions you researched and quiz each other! Dinner, drinks, and fun times optional, but of course, highly recommended as part of this activity.

Research other jobs

I know it's obvious that this could transform your career, but you'd be surprised how many people neglect this step and instead opt to complain about their current job.

And here's the thing, it's not so much about applying for the jobs you find as it is about opening your eyes to the many wonderful possibilities that are out there. We spend so much time heads down at work, never thinking or dreaming or daring to hope for better. And that's a shame, because there are tons of cool jobs out there, many of which you would enjoy a LOT more than what you're doing today.

Here's the thing about researching other jobs. It changes something within you when you do it. Even if you never apply. Even if you do apply and they turn you down.

Sometimes, we're stuck thinking that the only thing we could possibly do is exactly the job we have today and that's simply not true. We've talked about the fact that change is hard and often our brains work against us by giving us reasons not to change. Brains are great at this trick! It usually shows up in the form of fear and the stories the brain tells us. Stories like:

You aren't qualified for that job. Don't even bother applying.

Your life is too busy right now to add this new thing.

No one will be impressed with that last project you worked on.

You're too old/tired/disorganized/whatever to do this.

Sound familiar? It definitely should! Here's the exciting part, though. Once you apply to a job, it breaks through the fear and your brain starts to see possibilities. You imagine yourself working somewhere else. You see how there just might be more than one option for you. You begin to consider ways to put your strengths and superpowers to work. And then your brain starts to see more opportunities and get creative. You break through the barrier that was holding you back and then you can build momentum around how to approach those things that aren't working for you in your current job.

The added bonus of doing job research is that you may discover that your current pay is under market value. This is a great chance to have a conversation with your boss about getting paid more. And who doesn't want that?

#PositiveAction to try, continue or expand

- Go to a job search board such as Indeed, Glassdoor, or LinkedIn and type in keywords that would be fun for you. Love the outdoors and hiking? Try each of those as search terms and see what comes up. Love knitting? Search on that. You'd be surprised how many hobbies actually have options for doing some form of paid work.
- When you find a job that piques your interest, do some actual research on it. What sort of education or training does a person with that job have? What career experience is needed? You can take a class or find a mentor to learn more.
- What is the pay range for your current job? You can leverage the job search boards and a simple

internet search ("*job title* salary near me"). Research to see where you fall within the pay range. Then plan accordingly (including practicing) to have a conversation with your boss if you're outside the range.

Develop a good relationship with your boss

Maybe your team is fine, but your boss is a nightmare! If I had a nickel for every time I worked for, or knew someone who worked for, a boss that wasn't living into the definition of what a good manager should be, I could build a very nice house with a wonderful view from atop my mountain of nickels.

I know you shouldn't have to step up and act like a grown-up when your boss can't. You're right. It's not fair. In fact, it kinda sucks. And yet, here we are. You can't control your boss, so if you want to create change it will take positive action on your part.

Here's why you may want to go through the effort. Your boss has more direct control over your work life than almost anyone else (except you, of course) so you will want to be on good terms with this person. They often give out all the work assignments, both good and bad. When you're on good terms with your boss, it increases your chances of getting a good assignment. This makes your work life much easier!

Another strong motivator is the fact that your boss is often in charge of monetary rewards like raises, bonuses, and promotions. I'm not suggesting you suck up simply for the money, but it may be worth the time and effort it takes to build a positive relationship with this person if more money for you is the end result. Last time I checked, very few people are independently wealthy. That means we go to work because we need the money. So get more of your share!

Also, your boss is busy. Your whole team is busy. Everyone in your company is busy. Except for that one person that's always hanging around the water cooler/cafeteria/coffee shop/neighbor's cubicle. Every company has at least one of these people. We won't dive down the rabbit hole of why, but I'm sure you've got a clear image of someone in mind right now. So where were we? Ahhh yes, people are busy.

Your boss is so busy, they may or may not have time to know exactly what you're working on. Or what you're interested in. Or what you'd really like to be doing with your time. And the only way for them to find out is for you to tell them. That's right. Have regular conversations with your boss about what you're enjoying and not enjoying. Talk about the things at the company you're interested in. Share where you're hoping to head next from a career standpoint. Your boss needs to know this in order to do their job well, so the next time a great assignment that is perfectly suited for you comes up, you're the one they think of assigning it to.

So at this point, you might be rolling your eyes because this advice would have been helpful to you a week/month/year/I-hope-not-longer ago, but now it's too late. You and your boss don't see eye to eye. I hear you!

I've been there… and it sucks. And yes, your boss

SHOULD be the one to cultivate a great relationship with you. And yes, your boss SHOULD try to relate to you, regardless of how they feel about you. And yes, your boss SHOULD be a great manager, mentor, and leader. Isn't it interesting all the bad feelings that arise when *should* is involved?

Let's face it. Bosses are people. And sometimes people can't or don't do their best work for a variety of reasons, some of which are obvious, and some of which are not. Regardless, it's never too late to fix a damaged relationship, but the hard work of this may fall onto you to make it happen (unfair, but true... just like many things in real life!).

You can start by acknowledging the awkwardness between you by saying something to the effect of, *"I feel like we've gotten off to a rough start..."* or *"I feel like we aren't working as effectively together as we could..."* The only way to start over is to talk about where you're both at and identify what expectations each of you isn't meeting. Then set an agreement to do better going forward.

Of course, there's always a chance you can't fully repair the broken relationship. You have no control over how your boss is going to act. But you can control you and make an honest effort to improve. Regardless of the outcome, celebrate the fact that you took positive action to fix things and for living into your version of your best self!

#PositiveAction to try, continue or expand

- Acknowledge the awkwardness – saying it out loud will probably give both of you some relief!
- Ask your boss for suggestions on how you can work more effectively together. It might be a simple adjustment you can make that has a dramatic impact on your quality of life and your relationship.
- Find someone who has a good relationship with your boss and observe their behavior. What do they do differently? If you know this person and are comfortable discussing the issue with them, ask them for advice.
- Reach out to your tribe and ask for advice on how to handle a relationship with a challenging co-worker. You don't have to reveal that this person is your boss. You may be surprised to discover that many people have walked this road before you and have excellent tips for what to do (and not do!).

6

THOSE WHO ACT

"Things do not change; we change." – Henry David Thoreau

As I've mentioned, I've read plenty of books with great advice. Unfortunately, I didn't always put that advice into practice. I know the same will be true for some of you.

But to those brave individuals willing to try to create a different path for themselves, to those brave enough to re-architect their life and world of work, I salute you. Change is never easy, but here's one thing I've learned the hard way: you won't regret taking positive action.

All the not-so-positive, unproductive behaviors share one thing in common. Regret. That shameful feeling that you've wasted precious time, money, and resources, all to end up in the exact same place as before with the added pain of feeling worse about yourself and your job situation. It's enough to make you want to throw up in your mouth. I know it was for me!

Positive action is the antidote to regret. It shifts your focus onto the abundant possibilities and away from the things your job lacks. It puts you back in the driver's seat by taking action to transform those things you can control while letting the rest go. Be smarter than me, sooner than me and pick a positive action to make changes today!

Positive action can transform us in myriad ways, if we are willing to let it. You see, positive action is contagious. It builds upon itself. Once you start down the path of positive action, you will want to continue because you finally see progress in the areas of your work and life where you've felt stuck.

That was absolutely my experience. It started with me focusing on my health. I kept adding new health-related positive actions every week until I began to feel good. Once I started to recognize the person I saw in the mirror again, I began to work on clarity regarding my job. Prior to that point, my brain had been in a fog and I couldn't quite figure out those things that hadn't been working for me in my job. The clarity helped me determine the next step from there. Then the next. And the same will be true for you.

The last thing I want anyone to feel after reading this book is overwhelmed. You can start in any area of your work or life you want to transform, pick a small positive action and get started. For me, I had a lot of possible areas I could have started with, but the one impacting me most negatively was my health, so that was how I decided where to start. For you, it may be talking with your boss, watching less to read more, or finding a class that sounds interesting. No one person's career journey is the same as anyone else's. Neither is the journey to get unstuck and out of misery.

This is where your Positive Action Plan comes in. It becomes the way for you to decide for yourself where to start. You likely already knew it, deep down inside. It also becomes the way to hold yourself accountable for doing the steps you need to in order to change.

This is the confirmation you've been waiting for, the sign to get started on the path to making lasting change. You get to choose every day if you want to continue to live and work in misery or if you will do something different today to get a different result.

Here's the other great thing about our choices. Each choice you make is doing one of two things. It is either bringing you closer to your authentic, amazing self or it is bringing you further away from there. If you haven't been paying attention to your authentic self, you may wonder if you are getting closer to or further from that goal. I know I did! But there will come a moment where you'll choose to do something (or choose to stop doing something) and you will feel it deep within you. You will know that the choice you just made brought out more of your authenticity. It's such an amazing feeling and you will deliberately seek it out more! And so goes the virtuous cycle.

Every day we must make a choice: Will I take positive action to achieve my Aspirations? If yes, decide what the right next step is for you and begin again. Each day, each hour, each minute, we can decide that we're ready to take positive action!

The path is simple, but it's far from easy. We already know the right thing to do, most of the time. The challenge lies in being Consistent and choosing the positive action. It's something that I continue to have to work on daily, so don't be surprised if the same is true for you. It can feel easier sometimes to do nothing, to not take action. But doing nothing will only get you where you are, not where you want to be.

That's why Targeted action is so important. We can change everything... just not all at the same time. It starts with one thing.

Of course, that one thing must be something that brings you closer to your Identity. It helps you live into the best version of yourself. It's aligned to your values.

We know that entire books have been written on the importance of why, which is the reason your action must be On Purpose. There's no way any of us will manage to be Consistent without a compelling why driving us.

Then it's time for the Next Step. And the next. And the one after that. The wonderful cycle of ActionAssessAdjust never ceases to amaze me in its simplicity and effectiveness. And suddenly, you've gone and done that thing that started as an Aspiration!

Regardless of where you're at in your career and life journey, there are myriad ways to improve and truly transform your job and life. It starts with the belief in something better and the faith that the small actions will add up over time.

The world is waiting for each of us to become the best

version of ourselves. Farewell, misery! Let's chart a new course together. We can change authentically through positive action, so let's get out there and create something better! I'm counting on you to be smarter than me sooner than me…

THANK YOU

Thank you for reading! I hope you found this helpful and took positive action by incorporating the strategies discussed into your job search. If you enjoyed this book, please consider leaving a five-star review. You can use this link:

WorkAuthentically.com/ReviewChangeAuthentically

I know you're busy and I genuinely appreciate your time. Your review can help others find this book, in addition to supporting me.

With gratitude,
Ally

ACKNOWLEDGMENTS

I guess you enjoy reading as much, or more, than I do! Welcome! I would first like to acknowledge you, the reader, for continuing to the very end. What a fine reward for you, to be acknowledged in a book! By all means, humblebrag to your friends and family about this moment where you were thanked publicly in writing. Better yet, buy them a copy so they can enjoy this unique privilege too!

I had writing a book on my I'd-like-to-do-that-someday list for 20 years. Here's to me for taking positive action to make that Aspiration a reality! Of course, if we're going to talk reality then here's a list of people who truly deserve credit.

To my wonderful family, who supported me as my fuzzy vision came into focus and who helped me create the time and space I needed for this endeavor. It is not lost on me all the effort spent by you in my absence. Your love and generosity know no bounds! Thank you.

To Bruce and Jenny for your support, encouragement

and honesty all these years. Thank you. I most appreciate your ability to call bullshit on any excuses I've had. You know I'll gladly do the same for you!

To Eva, Dana, and Sherill, who provided insightful commentary and made this creation worth publishing. Thank you.

To my launch team, who willingly gave of their time and talents in service of putting something original out into the universe. Thank you.

ABOUT THE AUTHOR

About the Author

Ally Bubb combines authenticity, honesty, and fun into her work as a career coach and speaker, helping people create career transformation by teaching them to tell compelling career stories. She knows all too well what it's like to be miserable in a job you hate and she's on a mission to help others discover the radical difference it makes for employees and employers when we all work authentically. In her free time, Ally is an avid reader, hiker, and documentary film watcher. She lives in the United States with her spouse and 2 children.

About Work Authentically

Work Authentically bridges the "misery gap" between employees and employers by teaching people to reinvent the world of work by leveraging their unique style, approach, and way of being. Work Authentically offers presentations, workshops, and individual and group coaching focused on careers, including personal brand, resumés, LinkedIn, and job search strategies. If positive action sounds like the thing you or your company have been missing, contact us at WorkAuthentically.com and sign up for our free newsletter to learn more!

BOOKS BY ALLY BUBB

Change Authentically: A Guide to Transform Your Job and Life Through Positive Action

Get Out of Your Pajamas, Take a Shower, and Talk to Someone: Job Searching During a Pandemic, Economic Downturn, Recession, or Other Crisis

NOTES

1. CURMUDGEONS AND OTHER MISERY

1. **References**
   Clifton, J. (2017, June 13). *The World's Broken Workplace*. Retrieved from The Chairman's Blog: https://news.gallup.com/opinion/chairman/212045/world-broken-workplace.aspx
2. Dictionary, R. H. (1995, May 14). *Definitions*. Retrieved from Dictionary.com: https://www.dictionary.com

2. POSITIVE ACTION

1. Oxford. (2019). *Definitions*. Retrieved from Lexico Dictionary Powered by Oxford: https://www.lexico.com/en
2. Oxford. (2019). *Definitions*. Retrieved from Lexico Dictionary Powered by Oxford: https://www.lexico.com/en

4. POSITIVE ACTION FOR LIFE

1. McAlary, B. (2018). *Slow: Simple Living for a Frantic World*. Sourcebooks.
2. Spaeder, K. (2019, November 27). *Will Walking 20 Minutes a Day Help Me Lose Weight*. Retrieved from Livestrong.com: https://www.livestrong.com/article/410839-will-walking-20-minutes-a-day-help-me-lose-weight/
3. Fritz, J. (2019, June 24). *Nonprofit Organizations: Volunteers: 15 Unexpected Benefits of Volunteering That Will Inspire You*. Retrieved from The Balance Small Business: https://www.thebalancesmb.com/unexpected-benefits-of-volunteering-4132453